YOUR KNOWLEDGE HAS VALUE

Bibliographic information published by the German National Library:

The German National Library lists this publication in the National Bibliography; detailed bibliographic data are available on the Internet at http://dnb.dnb.de .

Imprint:

Copyright © 2006 GRIN Verlag, Open Publishing GmbH
Print and binding: Books on Demand GmbH, Norderstedt Germany
ISBN: 9783668275775

This book at GRIN:

http://www.grin.com/en/e-book/338122/analysis-of-chapter-lxvii-from-william-makepeace-thackeray-s-novel-vanity

Nadine Schneider

Analysis of chapter LXVII from William Makepeace Thackeray's novel "Vanity Fair"

GRIN Publishing

GRIN - Your knowledge has value

Since its foundation in 1998, GRIN has specialized in publishing academic texts by students, college teachers and other academics as e-book and printed book. The website www.grin.com is an ideal platform for presenting term papers, final papers, scientific essays, dissertations and specialist books.

Visit us on the internet:

http://www.grin.com/

http://www.facebook.com/grincom

http://www.twitter.com/grin_com

Universität Siegen

Sommersemester 2006

Love and Money

Analysis

of chapter LXVII

from *Vanity Fair*

Term Paper

Nadine Schneider

Analysis of chapter LXVII from *Vanity Fair*

I.   Introduction: From a thousand thoughts to *Vanity Fair*

"There are a thousand thoughts lying within a man that he does not know
till he takes up a pen to write."

(William Makepeace THACKERAY)[1]

And a thousand thoughts - or perhaps even some more - were probably the reason why Thackeray's *Vanity Fair* became such a large piece of work. Undoubtedly, the novel belongs to the most ambitious literary works of Victorian Age. However, this status is due not only to its remarkably large extent stored on almost a thousand pages[2] but also to its tartly depicted content, in short: love, money and power.

William Makepeace Thackeray at first published his work as a series in the London satire magazine *Punch* from 1847 till 1848. In regard to the piece's exceptional length this method of releasing was probably the easiest for the readers as thus they had the possibility to successively become acquainted with the protagonists of the story. And as a matter of fact a literary work of such a length comes up with more than only a few figures as well as it features a plot which is not free of slight inconsistencies and blemishes.

But not these light formal stains characterize *Vanity Fair* but the faults and failures that are made by the protagonists and which uncover the true nature of mankind. And as there are not only a few 'human stains' to be found but rather lots of, the reader is gliding through a story of bedazzling and betraying, cheating and corrupting, until in the very end all lies and secrets will be disclosed.

Probably, Rebecca "Becky" Sharp is the most controversial person in *Vanity Fair*. Throughout the book she seems to have only one goal: achieving a high rank within society and enjoying wealthy and luxury. But in spite of her wickedness and bewitching attacks on rich men she must early experience that life cannot be planned and that setbacks are unpleasant but possible.

The other female protagonist, Amelia "Emmy" Sedley, is the complete opposite of Rebecca. Not a high social status she longs to conquer but a man with whom she can outlive her romantic feelings. At first it appears as if she has found this specific fellow but the perils of destiny - and also

---

1   http://thinkexist.com/quotes/william_makepeace_thackeray/
2   varies from edition to edition

infidelity - ruin her marriage.

These two women stand as examples for two completely different beliefs: Becky only trusts in monetary values, whereas Emmy's true salvation lies in love and loyalty – but also in religion and faith.

In how far the marriage between Amelia and George Osborne could be considered a true love relationship is not the main subject of this analysis. I will rather examine why Amelia has such problems to couple with another man and prove that she actually has strong feelings for someone.

Moreover, on the example of her capturing Joseph Sedley I will take a closer look at Rebecca's hunt for prestige.

Furthermore, I will compare the two women and eventually analyze which role the story's narrator has.

Since the novel on the whole is too large to overlook, my analysis will concentrate on the very last chapter "Which Contains Births, Marriages, And Deaths".

II.   Analysis: Parasitism or Women on the hunt for life

1.   Brief outline of what happened to Amelia and Rebecca over the years

Vanity Fair takes places during the Napoleonic Wars. Altogether the story line is stretched over circa twenty years. In this time many things happen:

Amelia gets married to George Osborne. For her it is a true love relationship, she even worships her husband as a national hero who seems to be free of faults. In fact, he does make mistakes, especially in regard to his marriage. Amongst other things, he betrays Amelia with Rebecca and wants to run away with her. Thus it cannot be assumed that he loved Amelia as much as he loved him. It was rather George's friend William Dobbin who made him marry her to keep his promise. But the marriage turns out to be ill-fated: While Amelia is pregnant with his child, George dies at war. For her and 'little George' hard times begin in which she is not only suffering from financial problems but also from her mourning for George and her loneliness.

Dobbin, who once was responsible for the coupling of Amelia and George, becomes her supporter at these difficult times. That he himself is in love with her for a long time cannot distract

Amelia, not even many years after George's death when she is suffering from seemingly endless grief.

Mournfulness is nothing Rebecca knows. Different from Amelia she is searching for money, might and mastery. From her first appearance in the novel until the very end she discloses much self-esteem and the constant, unbreakable will to achieve a higher social standing than she actually has. So she tries to couple with men of high status. At first she wants to attract Joseph Sedley, Amelia's elder brother, and almost succeeds. Joseph is in fact interested in her but a potential marriage is denied by the intervention of Amelia's later husband George Osborne. In the following Rebecca marries Rawdon Crawley but cannot profit from the commitment as he gets disinherited after the match. Becky begins some affairs and tries to make money with them but is discovered by Rawdon who thereafter separates from her. But she does not suffer much from the divorce as well as she is not hurt when not seeing her child, 'young Rawdon', any more.

2.   Amelia

Taking a closer look at Amelia her sadness turns out to be more than mere mourning for a dead one: Although it first appears that never again emotions for another man could establish in Amelia, especially the last chapter of *Vanity Fair* discovers how deeply her yearning for William Dobbin is. For example, in conversations with her son she shows her opinion of the man: "She told him that she thought Major William was the best man in all the world; the gentlest and the kindest, the bravest and the humblest." (p. 659) In fact, she even uses her child as a 'transmitter' to stay in contact with him:

> "**She made George write to him** constantly, and persisted in sending **Mamma's kind love** in a postscript. And as she looked at her husband's portrait of nights, it no longer reproached her- perhaps she reproached it, now William was gone." (p. 659)

Why she is fighting these feelings can be explained by considering her attitude towards religion. As a pious Christian she feels obliged to love and adore her apparently decent and honourable husband, even posthumously, and although ultimately George's death happened over fifteen years ago. This inner conflict can be seen here:

> "Emmy defended her conduct, and showed that it was **dictated only by the purest religious principles**; that a woman once, &c., and to such an angel as him whom she had had the good fortune to marry, **was married for ever**; <u>but she had no objection to hear the Major praised</u> as much as ever Becky chose to praise him; and <u>indeed brought the conversation round to the Dobbin subject a score of times every day</u>." (p. 658)

This text passage can be subdivided into two different parts: The first is about Amelia's bonding to George, even after his death, the second treats her feelings for Dobbin which are factually there but only outlived passively, by enjoying talks about him.

Amelia's religiousness is shown once more when she finds books and gloves from Dobbin and stores them neatly but secretly:

> "Emmy cleared these [volumes] away, and put them on the drawers, where she placed her **work-box, her desk, her Bible, and Prayer-book, under the pictures of the two Georges**. And the <u>Major</u>, on going away, having left his gloves behind him, it is a fact that Georgy, rummaging his mother's desk some time afterwards, found <u>the gloves neatly folded up, and put away</u> in what they call the secret drawers of the desk." (p. 659)

Again the excerpt shows an ambivalent tendency: Amelia lives according to religious principles – the Bible and Prayer-book are symbols of her belief whereas the work-box could be seen as a tool to distract her thinking and feeling from Dobbin. At that time Christians lived on rules which should restrict the individual's own thinking and desiring. The two pictures underline these moral restrictions – they shall remind her of being loyal towards George and absent from William. That Dobbin is nevertheless permanently on her mind, if only unconsciously, is symbolized by his books and gloves – these are part of the desk, even though they are hidden.

It seems that Amelia does not want to change this situation. She seems unable to realize that at the same time William - in addition to their current spatial separation - desires to abandon his affection for her:

> "<u>He loved her no more</u>, he **thought**, *as he had loved her*. He never could again. That sort of regard, which he had proffered to her for so many faithful years, can't be flung down and shattered, and mended so as to show no scars. [...]; had she been worthy of the love I gave her, she would have returned it long ago. It was a fond mistake." (p. 662)

Similar to Amelia also Dobbin shows ambivalent tendencies: On the one hand he **thinks** that his love has changed, on the other hand already the mere fact that he thinks about Amelia shows that he still feels a lot for her. But there is something else in this passage that is remarkable: The arrangement of the statement. Dobbin's first sentence is in such a way arranged that the reader at first thinks that he "loved her no more", that his appreciation vanished. But by reading the entire sentence it becomes clear, that he is of the opinion that only the level of his love has changed – at least he thinks, but apparently not knows, this.

Nevertheless, William Dobbin is deeply frustrated of Amelia's continuous rejection and wonders if she is "worthy of the love" he has offered her.

At the time when the Major has such ambivalent thoughts Emmy has a premonition of what is going on:

> "[Dobbin sent letters] **so unconstrainedly cold** that the poor woman felt now in her turn that she had lost her power over him and that, as he had said, he was free. He had left her, and she was wretched. The memory of his almost countless services, and lofty and affectionate regard, now presented itself to her and rebuked her day and night. She brooded over those recollections according to her wont, saw the purity and beauty of the affection with which she had trifled, and reproached herself for having flung away **such a treasure**." (p. 662)

Here the full dimension of Amelia's feelings for Dobbin is depicted: She is afraid that she could have lost "such a treasure" whose letters have become "so unconstrainedly cold".

Already before Rebecca's intervention Emmy decides to send him a letter with the request that he might come back to her. But not till Becky tells her about George's plans of abandoning her, Amelia's eyes open up and the burden of eternal obligation to her unfaithful husband is taken away: "'There is nothing to forbid me now,' she thought. 'I may love him with all my heart now. Oh, I will, I will, if he will but let me and forgive me.'" (p. 666)

In the end, there is a relieved and happier Amelia who has another child and is content with her new marriage to Dobbin.

3.   Rebecca

Different from Amelia Rebecca does not have problems with emotional conflicts. Instead, in the last chapter of the novel she continues something that she has already started at the beginning of the novel:

Again it is Joseph, now even wealthier, who becomes the object of her desire. To win him for her own purposes she tries to overwhelm him with compliments and evokes the impression that he means much to her by using the purchase of a picture for a spectacle: "'I bought it,' said Becky in a voice trembling with emotion; 'I went to see if I could be of any use to my kind friends. I have never parted with that picture – I never will.'" (p. 661) Joseph seems to be deeply impressed by her show, so much that "he did not sleep, for a wonder, that night, any more than Amelia" (p. 661), and gets more and more caught by the woman. Finally, "she had cast such an anchor in Jos now as would require a strong storm to shake. That incident of the picture had finished him." (p. 664)

Even if the two do not marry, Rebecca can profit from the relationship in respect of the fame and the money she can exploit.

In the end she has not found a love but apparently never searched one but obtained a place in her *Vanity Fair* – for the church she acts in the role as a rich lady who organizes charity events:

> "[…] Rebecca, Lady Crawley, chiefly hangs about Bath and Cheltenham, **where a very strong party of excellent people** consider her to be a <u>most injured woman</u>. […] She busies herself in works of <u>piety</u>. She <u>goes to church</u>, and never **without a footman**. Her name is in all the <u>Charity Lists</u>. The Destitute Orange-girl, the Neglected Washerwoman, the Distressed Muffinman, find in her a fast and generous friend. She is always having stalls **at Fancy Fairs** for the benefit of these <u>hapless beings</u>." (p. 672)

Here it is eye-catching how contradictory Rebecca's later life is: On the one hand she mainly enjoys being part of "excellent people" while on the other hand she has to mess around with poor people, with the "hapless beings", to make a name for herself and be put onto the "Charity Lists". The insertion of the "Distressed Muffin-man" ironically hints at her still having affairs with diverse men.

4.   Differences of Amelia and Rebecca in their style of speaking and its consequences

The discrepancy between Amelia and Rebecca is not only marked by their completely different aims of life but also by their behaviour and speech. Rebecca's habitual language use is very direct and ungentle, for example when saying,

> "She must go away, the **silly little fool**. She is still **whimpering** after that **gaby** of a husband-- dead (and served right!) these fifteen years. […]You must have a husband, you **fool**; […] you **silly, heartless, ungrateful little creature**!" (p. 665),

Amelia generally tends to express herself in a more complicated way. Unlike Becky Emmy does not automatically say what she really thinks or wants. For all that, the reader learns to interpret Amelia's way of speaking and condensate what she really wishes. A good example is her strong desire for William Dobbin which can be realized primarily by her repetitive talking about him. Apparently, she enjoys making his name a recurring subject of conversations, but avoids to say why she likes talking about him, probably ashamed of disclosing what she really feels for him.

That Amelia actually has very strong feelings for Dobbin can be better seen at the moment he returns after Amelia sent for him. Here she kisses one of his hands, touches his breast, murmurs nervous fragments and then asks him if he will ever again leave her (cf. p. 668).

But even if the final chapter shows a successful union of Amelia and Dobbin, their relation appears to be lacking of the ultimate happiness. Perhaps Amelia's long lasting ignorance towards Dobbin has left its traces – short before his return he had distancing thoughts on Amelia (see above). That he later donates his love and free time rather to his child than to Amelia could also be evidence that he has reduced his previous high emotions for the woman down to a more moderate level (cf. p. 672).

5.   The irony of the commenting narrator

Regarding the formal aspects of *Vanity Fair* Thackeray has not left much room for the reader's own interpretation since the narrator mainly presents himself as an ironic omniscient commentator.

He finishes the last chapter with the words:

> "Ah! *Vanitas Vanitatum*! which of us is happy in this world? Which of us has his desire? Or having it, is satisfied? — Come, children, let us shut up the box and the puppets, for our play is played out." (p. 672)

In this final statement the narrator directly speaks to the reader and presents himself as the master of puppets. That he addresses his audience as "children" lifts him into the higher position of an adult, a teacher or an entertainer.

One more aspect of the excerpt is interesting: "Vanitas Vanitatum!" If this Latin exclamation would be translated with the words "Nothing is for eternity!" the comment could be a final hint at Dobbin's cooled-down emotions for Amelia.

Generally, the narrator often uses irony. When Rebecca visits the Sedleys in the last chapter he comments on her arrival like this:

"When a traveller talks to you perpetually about the **splendour of his luggage**, which he does **not happen to have with him**, my son, beware of that traveller! He is, ten to one, an **impostor**. – **Neither Jos nor Emmy knew this important maxim.**" (p. 660)

Once more the narrator seems condescent, like an advisor. But what is more important: He blames Becky to be an "impostor" and alleges that Joseph and Amelia are too naïve to see.

Moreover, the narrator points out some other capacities and talents of the protagonists by adding own thoughts and ideas. It seems that nobody of the figures is really able to satisfy the high expectations of the narrator:

Amelia is on the one hand criticised as naïve, whiningly and too submissive towards her husband and religious rules but on the other hand called a "tender little parasite" (p.668) who feeds herself on Dobbin's appreciation and loyalty.

Rebecca seems to be an egocentric and calculating person who continuously goes after social recognition and monetary values – but there are rare moments in which she thinks of others, for example when she helps Amelia out of her emotional dilemma by telling her the truth about George.

Joseph, "a man who had seen [military] service" (p. 661) - but not provided it himself - appears as a self-fixed coward whose greatest capabilities seemingly lie in eating and drinking as well as in being admired by women – what most of the times is only happening in his own imagination or faked by intriguing persons like Rebecca.

Only Dobbin seems to be without bigger stains. But since the subtitle of *Vanity Fair* is *novel without a hero* he cannot be a real hero as well, probably because he is too obliged to care for Amelia's benefit and too little caring for his own sake.

III.   Conclusion: All things come to an end

Summing up it can be said that the last chapter from *Vanity Fair* leaves no open endings since all storylines come to a close:

Amelia finds a new man for life and regains happiness. Rebecca achieves high social standing. Dobbin and Joseph are the donators of the women's fortunes. Dobbin can profit from the marriage with Amelia and enjoy her new relieved appreciation for him and love the child she has born to him, but Joseph finally becomes another fatality of Rebecca's addiction of advancement.

Comparing the two female main protagonists in the last chapter it can be subsumed that although they differ in life aims and intentions they show similarities in their treatment of men:

Whereas the both of them seem to allure men, Becky hunts after those who are supportive for her career, specifically, while Amelia at first searches for a man for life, finds one and later tries to cope with his death and the posthumous obligations. To do so she uses Dobbin as the man she secretly adores but does not dare to love in public. The consequence is that he feels neglected and rejected, ignored and finally so frustrated that he apparently distances himself from Amelia.

Altogether, it must be resumed that Amelia is much more harmless than Becky because she does not act out of selfish motifs but because of piety, self-imposed personal obligation and the unquenchable desire for warmth, caress and love because:

> "It is best to love wisely, no doubt;
> but to love foolishly is better than not to be able to love at all."

> (William Makepeace Thackeray)[3]

---

[3]http://thinkexist.com/quotes/william_makepeace_thackeray/

IV.　Bibliography

Primary Literature:

Thackeray, William Makepeace. *Vanity Fair*. London: Penguin, 1994.

Additional Web Source:

ThinkExist.com. *Finding Quotations was never this Easy!*. 1999 – 2006. 2008.

http://en.thinkexist.com/

ThinkExist.com. *William Makepeace Thackeray*. 1999 – 2006. 2008.

http://thinkexist.com/quotes/william_makepeace_thackeray/